PRAISE FOR
DOCTOR, HEAL THYSELF

"Physician wellness is the key to overcoming adversity in life and career. Dr. Dianne has THE system in place to ensure physicians remain vital."

—Doctor Jarret Patton,
#1 bestselling author of *Licensed to Live:
A Primer to Rebuilding Your Life after
Your Career Is Shattered*

"Dr. Dianne is a key stakeholder in the lives of her clients. She works diligently to not only succor the physician who needs a revitalization in the area of wellness, but also to empower them to amplify their true voice. Dr. Dianne's system is proven and effective. This book is a must-read."

—Charmaine Gregory, MD, FACEP,
coauthor of *The Chronicles of Women in White Coats*
and *Thinking About Quitting Medicine, vol. 2*, emergency
physician, speaker, wellness champion, and coach

"A leader in physician wellness, Dr. Dianne uses her great resources of experience, insight, and compassion to guide her colleagues off the path to burnout toward careers and lives that they love. This is so important, not just for physicians personally, but for society overall. Unless we address physician wellness, we will continue to see many doctors, after having invested so much in education and training, fleeing medicine, contributing to our physician shortage."

—Dina D. Strachan, MD,
board certified dermatologist, consultant,
bestselling author, and speaker

"In this book, as it does in person, Dr. Dianne's talent shines through in healing the minds, bodies, and spirits of our physicians. Bridging the vital connections of self-care for doctors to patient care can be achieved with this great system!"

—Dr. Hodon Mohamed, OB-GYN,
resident wellness expert,
speaker, and author

Doctor, Heal Thyself

A Guide for Physicians to Prevent Burnout
and Promote Wellbeing

DIANNE ANSARI-WINN, MD, MPH

purposely
created
PUBLISHING

DOCTOR, HEAL THYSELF
Published by Purposely Created Publishing Group™
Copyright © 2019 Dianne Ansari-Winn

All rights reserved.

Printed in the United States of America

ISBN: 978-1-949134-98-8

Special discounts are available on bulk quantity purchases by book clubs, associations and special interest groups.
For details email: sales@publishyourgift.com
or call (888) 949-6228.

For information log on to:
www.PublishYourGift.com

This book is dedicated to the Spirit that lives in and lights up every molecule of this beautiful universe, and to all of the wonderful people with whom I have had the privilege to share part of my life, even if it was for only an instant. (If you are wondering if I mean YOU, the answer is yes.) May we all find peace in our lives and cherish each other.

TABLE OF CONTENTS

FOREWORD

From the first time I met Dr. Dianne, like most people who meet her, I was drawn in by her infectious smile, her gentle yet powerful intelligence, and her passion for serving others through her work with physicians. Of course, it wasn't surprising to meet someone of such a caliber in that setting, since we were both attending the Global Influence Summit, a conference for people who are committed to making a difference in the world. In getting to know Dr. Dianne, I also quickly learned about her passion for learning. She routinely invests time and money into improving as a person and a professional and shows her huge generosity in wanting to share everything she has learned with everyone who could benefit.

This is exactly what you get here! Years of investment (time, money, blood, sweat, and tears) are all boiled down into an easy-to-digest book that embodies Dr. Dianne's principles, strategies, and exercises. This is the juicy stuff she shares with those fortunate enough to hire her as a coach and that she has proven in the laboratory of her own life. That's right. She "walks her talk"—having gone through burnout herself and come out the other side battle-hardened and wiser. This is one of the many things that Doc Dianne and I have in common. As a fellow health practitioner, I've seen burnout and its devastating effects from both the inside and the outside for the past twenty-two years as a psychologist and speaker. Unfortunately, it's usually those of us that have a real passion for helping that get hit by burnout the hardest.

Doctor Dianne is committed to her physician clients, as well as to the entire physician community. Her mission is to improve healthcare overall by improving the health and wellbeing of doctors. She does this not only as a mentor to the next generation of physicians, but also as a coach, speaker, author, and host of *The Doctor's Life* podcast. As part of her mission, she founded the Physician Vitality Institute and The Physician Coaching Academy to better serve her colleagues and society at large.

Whether you are a doctor or not, you're going to get incredible value from this book. But don't just read it; share it with the people in your life—especially physicians and other healthcare professionals.

Enjoy,

Dr. Ganz Ferrance, PhD, internationally recognized clinical psychologist, and author of *The Me Factor: A Systematic Guide to Getting What the Hell You Want*

INTRODUCTION

I have always been a high achiever and a problem solver. I was the oldest of my siblings, learned to read when I was four, skipped a grade in elementary school, decided to go into medicine when I was thirteen, and started college at sixteen. Growing up, I was the one my friends went to when they had problems. Even my mom leaned on me when she needed support.

I attended University of Michigan as an undergraduate, and then went directly to University of Michigan Medical School, where I met a special classmate who would later become my husband. Our first date was on my twenty-first birthday. After my second year of medical school, I felt like I wanted to "take a break," so I obtained a master's degree in health behavior and health education. I then returned for my third and fourth year of medical school and graduated with a combined degree of MD/MPH.

After medical school, I did an internship in pediatrics at a very highly regarded program in Chicago. I got married after my internship year and went into anesthesia residency in Chicago, where I was chief resident. I completed a combined fellowship in pain management and cardiothoracic anesthesia while my husband was completing his chief resident year. We then moved to Denver, where I went into private clinical practice and my husband pursued his fellowships in pulmonary medicine and critical care medicine. Within five years I had made partner in my group, during which I had my son and then my daughter. Also during those five years, we purchased our starter house, then our second, bigger, "doctor" house. At that time, everything was going according to plan. I had my work, I had my doctor husband, I had two beautiful children, and I was living in a beautiful place; what could be better, right?

I was a great Anesthesiologist. I loved helping people and loved my connections with my physician colleagues, nurses, and patients. In addition, the work was really cool—and just scary enough to keep me interested. I was kind of an adrenaline seeker in my early days of medicine. That made it exciting at first, but then, as time went by, it kind of lost its cool aspect and just started to feel scary. I started to dread being called in when I was on call and would sometimes cry on the way to work before a big case. But I hid it. I didn't talk about it much—just sucked it up and kept going. I couldn't admit that all this was going on—I told myself that no one would understand. I was afraid that I might be censured in some way or lose my ability to practice, or at the very least not be trusted by the other doctors and nurses that I worked with. Again, I hid it. I internalized it and turned it in on myself. I thought there was something wrong with me.

You know what I really wanted to be doing? Talking with and connecting with the patients and my colleagues. I wanted to be a healer. I wanted to create transformation. My favorite service was obstetrics because I could connect with the patients; I could really be with the moms and help them. I was the doc that the other docs asked for when they wanted TLC for their patients. I talked the moms through their C-sections and held their hands. On the outside, I was such a success. On the inside, I didn't feel successful at all.

Fast forward to ten years later, which was June of 2012. It was a beautiful summer morning in Denver. The sun was shining and it was another perfect day in Colorado. It was my day off, and I should have been spending the day with my kids doing something fun. But instead, I was in the psychiatrist's office, crying. Again. We had been talking for several months at that point. I went to see a psychiatrist because I thought I had depression and because I wanted to talk with a fellow physician about

what doctors need to be healthy—and what I have come to know for sure is that my story doesn't have to be your story. You don't have to choose between practicing medicine and burnout. It doesn't have to be that way at all.

There is a way to have the capacity, energy, and vitality to do whatever you want in life, including practicing medicine if you want to do so, and that is what I teach my clients. I haven't had a client leave medicine yet, actually, and they are living the lives they want to live.

One thing that I have found is that doctors think they can manage on their own. But I have learned from recovering from burnout myself, and from coaching my colleagues who are suffering from stress and burnout, that having someone that can objectively guide you on your path to getting or staying healthy in mind, body, and spirit saves you so much time and effort, because they can help you identify where you are and guide you to where you want to go. I was there. I get it. And my clients appreciate that and feel safe.

Chapter 1

WHY CARING FOR YOURSELF IS CRITICAL

*You owe yourself the love that
you so freely give others.*

—Unknown

I've interviewed many doctors on my podcast *The Doctor's Life*. They share their stories of how they came to medicine and how they developed into the physicians that they are today. There are three common themes in these "origin stories." The first is that many of the doctors were mentored by a physician who inspired them to pursue medicine. The second is that they were "called" to medicine. And the third is that they gain deep satisfaction from service to others.

If you are a physician, it's critical to care for yourself because you care for so many others when you are practicing medicine. Physicians are givers, and it's in our nature to give. From medical school onward, we give of our time, by studying and learning, and our energy, by foregoing sleep, food, and our own health to care for our patients. We get great satisfaction from helping others and feel rewarded when we do. Part of the reason for the respect that doctors enjoy is that not everyone can do or is even willing to do the great work that physicians do. The work that physicians do—shepherding and safeguarding the health and wellbeing of patients, doing research, and teaching others our profession—is nothing short of heroic. However, we have to remember that while physicians do things that are heroic, and even do work that seems superhuman, we are not superhuman.

We are, indeed, simply human.

Paradoxically, the same profession that we love is taking its toll on many in the form of physician burnout. It is now well known that between 30 to over 50 percent of medical students, residents, and physicians in practice (depending on the specialty) are suffering from burnout in some form. As you are reading this, maybe you are that doctor. Physicians suffering from burnout are tired, cynical, disconnected, and lonely. They question their own ability to practice medicine. They are suffering from cardiovascular disease, excessive weight, stress, addiction, and failed relationships. They can be hard to work with. They are cutting back their hours and leaving practice altogether. It is well known that physician burnout not only has a negative effect on the one who suffers, it also adversely affects our relationships with our patients, their adherence to our instructions, their recovery from their illnesses, and the safety and quality of their care.

As you may have read in the introduction, I have personal experience with burnout. Leaving clinical medicine in June 2012 was one of the hardest things that I ever did in my life. From the time I was thirteen, medicine has defined me, and my experience with burnout has both refined and redefined me. The process of becoming a physician and practicing medicine for fifteen years as an Anesthesiologist in private practice—literally dealing with life-and-death decisions on a daily basis—has had a major defining role in who I am today. Even now I am dedicated to our physician community as a coach for physicians and as a founder of a school where I teach physicians coaching skills, because I believe that physicians are some of the best people in the world. I say this without any pride—this is my honest observation. Physicians are some of the most kind, loyal, and self-sacrificing people on this Earth. It is my personal mission to help physicians have their best lives—that means you Doctor!

If we want to work to our fullest potential, it's important to keep our bodies healthy, and our health depends on taking care of ourselves. As physicians, we should know this better than anyone, right? But taking care of ourselves involves more than just avoiding things that are directly harmful to our bodies, such as drinking, smoking, substance use, overeating, and other harmful behaviors. In addition to not doing our bodies harm, we as physicians in particular need to keep our bodies healthy because of the important work that we do, and because our work is inherently stressful. If we don't take care of our bodies through adequate rest, sleep, exercise, and diet, we can find ourselves facing a host of negative consequences. We can suffer from illnesses that we might be predisposed to, but could have prevented the development of, such as hypertension, coronary artery disease, and diabetes. We can suffer from stress-related illnesses such as obesity, adrenal fatigue, and autoimmune diseases. We can also be more susceptible to cancer. And, very importantly, we can be more susceptible to mental illnesses. Depression and anxiety can be more common when our bodies and minds are stressed out.

If you get exhausted from life's trials without replenishing yourself through self-care, then you can lose the most important and rejuvenating part of life—relationships. Our relationships help make our lives rich in mind, body, and spirit. If you do not care for yourself, your relationships will suffer. You won't have the capacity to give to patients, colleagues, friends, family, partners, and spouses what they need from you. Being in a relationship with a physician can be a challenge in many ways, and one of those challenges is that we are stretched thin. Quality time with the people we love is so important for us and for them. If we don't have the capacity to give to others because we are running on fumes ourselves, everyone loses.

If you don't care for yourself, you won't have the energy and capacity to accomplish what you want to in your lifetime. What do you want your legacy to be? Would you like to be successful in your work, and work for as long as you would like to be able to? Would you like to be an involved and energetic parent? Would you like to be a kind, loving, and compassionate partner? Would you like to live with optimum health? Would you like to be financially successful?

There is a misconception amongst doctors that pursuing health and wellness is for other people, or that if we do pursue it, we are chasing an unrealistic goal, or that it is frivolous in some way. We may even think that doctors who want to be healthy aren't as serious or committed. But I actually think that ignoring one's health is being unrealistic and foolhardy. People outside of medicine easily see this, but somehow we don't see it as well. We have a huge blind spot when it comes to our own health. Our culture rewards us for doing things that are hard—and that's okay. But we need to recognize that because our work IS hard, we need to have a plan to take care of ourselves so that we can have the careers and lives that we want.

Chapter 2

YOU AS THE PRIORITY IN YOUR LIFE

An empty lantern provides no light. Self-care is the fuel that allows your light to shine brightly.

—Unknown

When I speak to groups or to my clients about putting ourselves first, I often receive a fair amount of resistance and pushback. It can feel selfish. Heck, sometimes even I feel some resistance about putting myself first. But it's a key component in developing and maintaining our optimal health in mind, body, and spirit. We are resistant because the conventional wisdom is that we should take care of others before we take care of ourselves. We have learned this from society at large, from our parents, and even from our colleagues in medicine. It's somehow considered to be heroic to put others first before ourselves. Now, it is fine at times to prioritize others over ourselves. However, when it becomes our default, or it starts to take too great a toll, the results can be discouragement, fatigue, apathy, overextension, and burnout.

Who successfully makes themselves a top priority? Successful leaders do! Whether they are leading a team of five people, a company of thousands of employees, or a country of millions of citizens, they know that in order for them to be strong and confident, and to have the capacity to hold a leadership role, they have to put themselves first so that they can be healthy in mind, body, and spirit. In addition, people who want to create their own lives—a rich life that's full of meaning, purpose, and joy—prioritize themselves, meaning that they understand who they are in the world, what is important to them, and how they can be with others in a healthy way.

Some might think that prioritizing ourselves actually takes away from our being able to fulfill our responsibilities to others. But actually it is a demonstration of our own personal responsibility, because taking care of yourself removes the burden from others to take care of you. It's actually very empowering; it shows others and ourselves that empowerment comes from within, not from the circumstances around us or from other people. It shows that we can co-create with others, live together, and cooperate with others in a loving way, without having other people be responsible for our own self-care and our own happiness. Prioritizing ourselves actually increases our ability to care for others, because we can help others more when our own cup is full. Taking care of ourselves first is also a way to be aware of ourselves and our wants and needs, so that we can truly care for ourselves in a loving way. It's actually an act of love, not only for ourselves but also for others.

Prioritizing ourselves allows us to stand up for ourselves. It gives us confidence. If we put ourselves first, then we can set boundaries around how we will and won't be treated. When we put ourselves first, we are not codependent on others to meet our needs, because we can meet our own needs. When we prioritize ourselves, we teach others how to treat us. If we are a parent and we prioritize ourselves, we are actually good examples for our children, because we give ourselves the capacity and strength to be there fully for them. We can make decisions that are good for them and good for us, without building up resentment or feeling like our time was not appreciated. We won't need appreciation to keep us going because we gave willingly after getting what we needed.

Prioritizing ourselves actually helps us to be more honest with others, more fully present with others, and more evolved ourselves. We can bring our best self to the world. Prioritizing ourselves is not negative or selfish. It allows others to really be with who we really are, not someone that we might be pretending to be. If we are at a point in our lives where we are in need of support and we don't have a lot of energy or time to give to others, then we can know that more clearly, because we have a better idea of who we are and what our wants and needs truly are at that time. We don't keep going and going based upon a false premise that if we give and give, we will be okay. Eventually we won't be okay. If we know who we are and what our boundaries are, when we say "yes," we are trusted that we really mean yes. And when we say "no," that is trusted and people really understand that we mean no as well.

Chapter 3

DISCOVERING (OR REDISCOVERING) YOUR PURPOSE

Our prime purpose in this life is to help others.

—attributed to the Dalai Lama

The first step in discovering (or rediscovering) your purpose is to identify your values. Identifying your values involves identifying what is important to you at your core. This means what moves you and what makes your heart glad. It may have been a while since you have considered this. It's really important to explore your core values, as they are the basis of not only what you do, but also who you are as a person. Our values define us, and they also guide us. We are dynamic beings and our core values can change over time, so it's important to identify them again now. Knowing your core values will also be useful to you as you go through the rest of this book.

As physicians, we tend to be very centered in our head, meaning we focus on our thoughts and intellect. While that serves us well in terms of getting things done, it doesn't serve us when it comes to identifying our purpose, because our purpose comes from our heart, soul, and spirit. Our purpose is our contribution to the world and is an expression of who we are. It helps us find our place in the world and make sense of the world. Listening to your heart is a different kind of process and will take different skills than our thinking skills. The beautiful thing is that, while listening to your heart takes some dedicated time, the "work" itself is easy and fun.

GETTING RID OF OTHERS' VOICES

Our purpose is our own. I believe that it is given to us by God, and has also been developed by our life experiences, both positive and negative. Interestingly, our purpose can change over time. Did you know that you don't have to have just one purpose? We can have different purposes that match the varied aspects of our lives. For example, we may have one life purpose be to raise our children well, and another life purpose be to serve mankind as a physician. Since our life purposes are unique to each of us, it is fundamental to quiet the influence of others when we are finding *our* purpose. It doesn't matter what you think you *should* be doing, because your purpose goes beyond thinking. If you are thinking about what you "should" do, you are likely off course. How do you know if you're hearing someone else's voice? You are if you're focusing on what others think about you or what others *will* think about you. If you are considering what your family, friends, colleagues, or society will think of you, you are not considering your purpose. Getting those other voices out of your head is key to finding your purpose.

EXERCISES

Here are four exercises to help you find your purpose. These exercises are best done over time, when you have some quiet time to sit with yourself and your thoughts without being interrupted. I hope you will be surprised and delighted at what bubbles up.

For each exercise, take a few minutes to be present with yourself and still your mind. Close your eyes and relax. Ask the question of the part of you that always knows the answers. Listen quietly, and then, when the voice within you starts revealing the answers, start writing without judgment or filter. Remember—you can't do this wrong!

EXERCISE #1:

1. Grab a pen and paper and set a timer for twenty minutes.

2. Dream about one of your favorite days of your life.

3. Write about that day. Why was that specific day one of your favorite days? What was happening? Who was with you? How did you feel?

4. Be specific about the three to five qualities that made that day your favorite.

You can write about several days, but that is not necessarily better. It's completely fine to go in depth into dreaming about and describing just one day in the twenty minutes that you have.

FAVORITE DAY #1

Description of the day:

_____

_____

What was special about that day?

_____

_____

FAVORITE DAY #2

Description of the day:

_____

_____

What was special about that day?

_____

_____

FAVORITE DAY #3

Description of the day:

_____

_____

What was special about that day?

_____

_____

When you are done, go back and read through what you have written. Again, be nonjudgmental and gentle here.

What do you see there? What would you like to bring forward? What does this tell you about what is important to you? What would you like to see more of?

_____

_____

EXERCISE #2:

Set a timer for at least fifteen minutes and write about:

What lights you up? What makes you happy?

_____

_____

When you are done, go back and read through what you have written. Again, be nonjudgmental and gentle here.

What do you see there? What would you like to bring forward? What does this tell you about what is important to you? What would you like to see more of?

EXERCISE #3:

Set a timer for at least fifteen minutes and write about:

What have you always been good at? This can include work, but also think about what people tell you you're good at, what people go to you for, and what you were talented at as a child.

_____

_____

When you are done, go back and read through what you have written. Again, be nonjudgmental and gentle here.

What do you see there? What would you like to bring forward? What does this tell you about what is important to you? What would you like to see more of?

EXERCISE #4:

Set a timer for at least fifteen minutes and write about:

Are there times in your life where you don't notice time passing by? What is happening during those times? Go into detail here . . . where are you? What are you wearing? Who is with you? What are you doing?

_____

_____

When you are done, go back and read through what you have written. Again, be nonjudgmental and gentle here.

What do you see there? What would you like to bring forward? What does this tell you about what is important to you? What would you like to see more of?

Chapter 4

ENERGY MANAGEMENT/ ENERGY RENEWAL

The key is not to prioritize what's on your schedule, but to schedule your priorities.

—**Stephen R. Covey,**
The 7 Habits of Highly Effective People

Energy renewal is the process of rejuvenating yourself in mind, body, and spirit. I base my work with my clients on the principles of energy management that I discovered in a *Harvard Business Review* article by Schwartz and Mc-Carthy from 2007. The idea is that you look at your life in terms of things that energize you and things that deplete you. It's common sense and proven with research. The benefits of managing your energy in a mindful way have been used with great success in the business community, and I love to share the principles of energy management with my clients. It's a real game-changer for them.

WHY IS ENERGY RENEWAL IMPORTANT?

Humans are designed to move rhythmically between spending and renewing energy. Some examples of this are sleep/wake cycles, physical energy cycles, and needing breaks after periods of intense concentration or problem solving. By recognizing these cycles and honoring them, we can get more done in less time, at a higher level of quality, and in a more sustainable way. Energy renewal increases our capacity to connect and feel connected with our purpose. It also increases our joy and our mental and physical energy.

In the original article, it was proposed that human beings require four sources of energy to operate at their best. However, in my work personally and with clients I find that there are five sources of personal energy that doctors need to cultivate, develop, and nurture to be at their most energetic and vital. Those sources of energy are connection to others, inspiration, emotional fitness, calming techniques, and caring for your body. All are necessary, and none of these sources of energy are sufficient by themselves.

Planning our day using energy management and energy renewal principles makes a lot of sense. Instead of just having tasks that have to be accomplished and motoring through several tasks that we know are going to take up a lot of energy, we can actually accomplish more with more joy and energy if we plan using energy management. We do this more or less intentionally when we plan vacation time and work time, and this concept can be used in just that way in our daily lives to effectively plan our days, weeks, months, and years.

I love using energy management because it takes away labels of things that are "work" vs. things that are "play," which are different for everyone. For example, I really like to do dishes. I like the warm soapy water, I like having my hands busy, I like being in the kitchen where my family tends to hang out, and I like the clean dishes and the satisfaction of having a job well done. I can imagine that some of you don't like to do dishes at all! But that task actually renews me somehow. It feels like a "work/break."

I invite you to start thinking of events, plans, and activities in terms of things that are depleting and things that are rejuvenating.

Here's an exercise to help you with this:

Grab a pen and paper and set a timer for twenty minutes. Now take a few minutes to be present within yourself and still your mind. Close your eyes and relax. Ask the question of the part of you that always knows the answers. Listen quietly and then, when the voice within you starts revealing the answers, start writing without judgment or filter. Remember—you can't do this wrong!

What are some things that energize you?

_____

_____

How do you feel when you are energized?

_____

_____

What are some things that deplete you?

_____

_____

How do you feel when you are depleted?

_____

_____

When you are done, go back and read through what you have written. Again, be nonjudgmental and gentle here.

What do you see there? What would you like to bring forward? What does this tell you about what is important to you? What would you like to see more of?

Chapter 5

THE PHYSICIAN VITALITY SYSTEM

There is a vitality, a life force, an energy, a quickening that is translated through you into action, and because there is only one of you in all of time, this expression is unique.

—Martha Graham

By now you are familiar with the importance of caring for yourself, putting yourself first, finding your purpose, and energy management/energy renewal. Now we are going to bring it all together in a system that I teach my clients—the Physician Vitality System. While my clients are primarily physicians, this system works well for anyone that is or wants to be a high-achieving person while still maintaining optimum health in mind, body, and spirit.

We have plans for continuing education, for our professional development, for research, and for retirement, but we tend to ignore ourselves in all of this. How are we going to have the energy to accomplish all that we want to? And for those of us who are feeling like we are already losing our momentum or have lost it entirely, how are we going to get it back? Through the Physician Vitality System.

The five fundamentals of the system are:

▶ Connection to Others: social connections with friends, colleagues, and family

▶ Calming Techniques: creating calm and relaxed concentration

▶ Inspiration: uplifting and nourishing our spirit

▶ Caring for Your Body: optimizing our body's health and function

▶ Emotional Fitness: diffusing negative emotions and cultivating positivity

The system addresses our whole lives, and each component is important to develop and nurture. However, it is well known by life coaches like myself, and others who are interested in personal development, that if one improves one aspect in their life, it undoubtedly will improve other aspects of their life as well. In the following chapters, we will explore the Physician Vitality System and see how you can use it for your life.

Let's go!

Chapter 6

CONNECTION TO OTHERS

They may forget what you said—but they will never forget how you made them feel.

—**Carl W. Buehner**

Our connections and relationships with others are one of the true joys of life. The people that we connect with get us through hard times and help us celebrate good times. They help us to grow and are mirrors for us. Through others, we live out our purpose. We will remember the people around us, and how we were with them, well after our careers are over. Human beings are social beings at our core. We know that social connections are key to our health and wellbeing. Studies have shown that being in isolation leads to depression and other physical illnesses. It is no surprise that physical isolation from others is used as torture and punishment. There is something within human nature that craves connection, that needs connection. Positive connections give us energy, purpose, and hope.

Studies have found that for physicians, some of the top indicators of happiness are related to our social connections. Sadly, and paradoxically, loneliness is silently rampant for physicians, who suffer from feeling lonely even though they are surrounded by people all day long. Physicians say that one of the reasons why they do not like electronic charting and short patient visits is that it takes away the connections that they develop with their patients. In addition, isolation is a hallmark of burnout. In medical groups and healthcare systems, opportunities for physicians to hang out, have lunch or dinner, or just talk have been shown to be immensely helpful for creating connections and improving morale at work.

So how do we create meaningful connections? The first step is to make our relationships a priority in our lives. We can make the mistake of making our social connections, our relationships with others, secondary to our work. However, our relationships are actually central to our health and our capacity to do our work. Our relationships with our families, partners, children, and friends are tremendously nourishing and rejuvenating, and they need tender loving care from us so that they grow and flourish. Our relationships are living things, just like plants. If they are ignored, they will struggle to survive, but with love and attention, they thrive.

The second step is to really be present with people when you are with them. That means paying attention to and really engaging with them. Sitting side by side doing parallel tasks with someone does not create a connection nearly as well as being present with people does. Of course, being with someone creates more of a connection than talking by phone does, which in turn creates more of a connection than texting does. If you have the choice, go for the greater connection. Reach for the phone instead of texting. Go talk to someone instead of calling. Both at work and at home, always try to go for the more personal connection.

Here are some ideas for creating closer connections:

At home—Turn off those electronics! They are such an easy distraction. Put down those phones, close your computer, and turn off the television.

With your partner—Create regular opportunities where you can spend time one-on-one, without kids.

Keep in mind that, in terms of importance, your relationship with your partner should actually take priority over the kids, because studies show that if you have a good relationship with your partner, then your kids will do better emotionally than if you do not. Come to agreements about parenting, especially if you have different parenting styles.

With your children—Really listen to them when they are talking and spend time with them doing things at their level. Play a board game. Cook together. Do errands or chores together. Have meals together as often as possible. For older children, you can learn so much when you are taking them to activities, because it's a time where you are all in the car together, and kids tend to share more in this casual environment. Take advantage of these opportunities.

With your extended family—If there are old rifts, try to overcome them; forgive and forget. A therapist can be helpful in this regard. Try to reach out from time to time if you are not close. If you are close to your extended family, use the principles noted above to try to make connecting with them a priority and to be present when you are connecting.

At work—As was mentioned before, creating an informal group to discuss things that are going on at work without it being a "staff meeting" is immensely helpful to create camaraderie and grow relationships. Getting together for an evening outing works wonders to bring coworkers together. Other ways to build relationships include trying to not have lunch alone, having annual or biannual picnics or dinners with colleagues and their families, and joining groups or committees at work, as well as being active in the local medical society.

Here's some ways to make some non-work friends:

▶ Attend group activities, such as group exercise classes, dance classes, or art appreciation

▶ Join spiritual or religious congregations or groups

▶ Organize or participate in group trips for those who wish to travel but do not have companions to travel with

▶ Get involved with the adults at your kids' school activities and sports

▶ Meet your neighbors! Form a neighborhood club or have a regular meet-up

▶ Attend a wellness retreat

▸ Join a Facebook group that has a local chapter—for example, I am a member of a doctor's Facebook group that meets locally.

Have fun!

Chapter 7

INSPIRATION

*When you are compassionate with yourself,
you trust in your soul, which you let guide
your life. Your soul knows the geography
of your destiny better than you do.*

—**John O'Donohue**

This part of the Physician Vitality System is where we focus on uplifting and nourishing our spirits, our souls, and our hearts. Inspiration comes from the Latin root *inspirare*, which means "to breathe into," which beautifully describes the solid yet ephemeral nature of connection with this vital part of our being. In Old English, inspiration means Divine Guidance. Regardless of your religious orientation or spiritual beliefs, developing this part of ourselves is a cornerstone in gaining and maintaining clarity, energy, focus, and purpose.

The connection with this part of ourselves is a deep well that we can always draw from for strength, for ideas, for guidance, and for reassurance. It is the part of us that is solid and true when our thoughts and feelings are all over the place. It is where our intuition lies. It is the collective consciousness and where inspiration comes from. We can be inspired by others, by places, by things, and by connecting with ourselves.

When we connect with our spirit, our soul, our heart, we feel grounded. It's a feeling of calm and well-being, of purpose, and sometimes of excitement. Our path forward feels clearer and more solid. Our fears and anxieties for the future tend to melt away. This is where we can find breakthroughs in our personal and professional lives and where we find solutions to problems that seemed tangled. Sometimes we get a sudden urge to do something or call someone that seems like it doesn't make sense, but if we follow through, we find it was the right thing to do. We go to that bakery we have always been wanting to try and see a friend that has been on our mind lately. We are inspired to get up a few minutes early and then experience something special—maybe hear a song, or spend a few minutes with our kid, or have a great idea that we would not have experienced otherwise. Following these connections can lead us to moments of surprise and delight.

When we are connected here, there is a feeling of timelessness, as though our time pressures are not as great. Time seems to expand in a way. We can become laser-focused and more efficient. There is a feeling of abundance, of love, of wholeness. We are present. If you did the exercises in the chapter on finding your purpose, reflect on your experience of doing those exercises. Do you notice any similarities from the description of connecting with this part of ourselves and what you experienced during the exercises?

TEN WAYS TO FIND INSPIRATION

These are in no particular order. Choose one and see what resonates for you. You may find, as I do, that you may develop or use several of these methods, depending on what is happening for you and what is available to you at the time.

1. Being in Nature: There is an aspect to being in nature that connects us and allows inspiration. This doesn't have to be a trip to the Grand Canyon. Taking a walk in your neighborhood, going

to a park, or going outside in your yard can work just as well. Breathe. Pay attention. Take off your shoes. Feel the wind. Listen to the birds or the human sounds around you. Touch the leaves on the trees.

2. Gratitude: This is one of the most-discussed ways of connecting with the spirit. Some people get stuck on the word "gratitude"—if that doesn't work for you, see if "appreciation" does. This can be done any time. Just take a few minutes, or even a few seconds, and simply appreciate what is going on. Here's some places to start: Appreciate that you are wearing clothes and shoes. Appreciate clean drinking water. Appreciate yourself!

3. Appreciation of Others: Spend a few minutes considering the connection of yourself to others—the most superficial connections (for example, the connections that it took with others to get this book into your possession) or the deeper connections that you have. This brings us into a feeling of wonder and marveling.

4. Meditation: This involves quieting our minds intentionally. When we get rid of our mental chatter and noise, it brings us to that deeper, calm,

creative place of inspiration. There are many ways to accomplish this—one is closing our eyes and belly breathing, as is described later on in this book. There are many types of meditation: silent meditation, meditation with sound, walking meditation, guided meditation, and more. I could write a whole chapter on meditation alone! I prefer silent meditation with breath, where you pay attention to your breath and belly breathing, and walking meditation, which for me is simply taking a walk outside without electronics, paying attention to everything in the present moment—breathing, how my body feels, the sounds and smells in the air, the weather—and focusing on those things in place of my thoughts.

5. Favorite Things: Do something, a favorite thing, that makes you lose track of time; take your pick. You may have to rediscover this! Is it a run? A hobby? Writing? Playing with your kids?

6. Affirmations: These are a powerful way of re-connecting with what you know to be true about yourself and your deeper nature—who you ARE, what you aspire to, and what you believe in. I find they are the most powerful if they are spoken out loud, even if only in a whisper. I have a list of

affirmations that I have collected and that I read daily, and I have several affirmations on sticky notes and a white board in my office. I am an incurable reader and I read everything around me, so I find that having affirmations around that I glance at and read often helps me to reconnect and get inspired. Here are five of my favorites:

» All of my worries of tomorrow are simply melting away.

» My life is a delicious series of connections and coincidences.

» I am the epitome of success at this moment.

» Today, something surprising and delightful will happen.

» Wherever I go, I leave little traces of goodness around me.

7. Reflection: Reflect on what has happened and what is happening in your life with curiosity and gratitude—not so much why things have happened, but that they have happened at all. When I reflect on how I got to this point—creating a book, which has been a dream of mine,

and working with physicians in the way that I do—I am amazed and humbled, and very deeply touched to the point of tears of gratitude.

8. Spiritual Practices: Prayer, meditation, reading sacred texts, being in congregation with others, and fasting are all ways to bring us closer to our souls and our hearts and to the Spirit.

9. Experiencing Beauty: It may be natural beauty, such as observing nature, or beautiful things that have been created by mankind, such as looking at art or architecture, listening to music, seeing a dance performance, or looking at photos of loved ones—but regardless of where it comes from, these experiences are rich and bring us inspiration.

10. Love: Last but not least, there is both receiving and giving love! Romantic love, self-love, love for others, love for an idea or a concept, love of a thing or a place—all of these can and do bring us inspiration and lift us up as individuals and as part of the human race.

I invite you to play with a few of these! What do you find works for you? Specifically, choose one, use it, and note your experiences here.

_____

_____

_____

_____

_____

_____

_____

_____

_____

_____

_____

_____

Chapter 8

CALMING TECHNIQUES

The quieter you become, the more you can hear.

—**Unknown**

This part of the Physician Vitality System is about creating calm and relaxed concentration. This is important because being able to be calm and relaxed during your day is key in managing your energy and not becoming frazzled and reactive to the events of the day.

In this chapter we are going to jump right into the techniques, and each technique will have an explanation as to why it works.

DIAPHRAGMATIC BREATHING WITH FOCUS

The first technique is diaphragmatic breathing with focus. This can be practiced anytime, anywhere, and is one of my favorite techniques. It is so simple and so effective! There have been a lot of descriptions on how to do belly breathing, but let's keep it simple. To do it, put one hand on your chest and one hand on your belly. Close your eyes and/or soften your gaze. Focus on taking breaths with your abdomen so that the hand on your stomach goes in and out. You can actually start doing this technique right now! Go ahead and take ten deep breaths this way. Then open your eyes and keep reading.

This type of breathing was made more popular in the West after Dr. Herbert Benson's book *The Relaxation Response* hit shelves in the mid-1970s. The benefits of this technique are:

Managing Stress: Our brains are routinely on high alert for threats in our environment—we're wired to react defensively to anything that hints of imperiling us physically or psychologically. We all know of the fight or flight response. When we are stressed or anxious, our bodies respond the same way, whether the threat is real or perceived. With this technique, we are creating a relaxation response in the body. Controlled breathing is one of the most effective ways of doing this.

Managing Anxiety: Belly breathing triggers the parasympathetic nervous system by stimulating the vagus nerve—a nerve running from the base of the brain to the abdomen, responsible for mediating nervous system responses and lowering heart rate, among other things. The vagus nerve releases a neurotransmitter called acetylcholine that catalyzes increased focus and calmness and smooths out the beat-to-beat variability in the heart rate. A direct benefit of more acetylcholine is a decrease in feelings of anxiety. Stimulating the vagus nerve may also play a role in treating depression, even in people who are resistant to antidepressant medications.

Lowering Blood Pressure and Heart Rate: Research suggests that when practiced consistently, controlled breathing will result in lower blood pressure and heart rate, which in turn results in less wear and tear on blood vessels. As described above, the vagus nerve plays a key role in this response. Beat-to-beat variability is also decreased, which is essential to heart health. Over time, using controlled breathing to lower your blood pressure and heart rate can help prevent strokes and can lower your risk of cerebral aneurysms.

Sparking Brain Growth: One of the more intriguing research developments involving controlled breathing is that when it's used to facilitate meditation, the result can be an actual increase in brain size. Specifically, the brain experiences growth in areas associated with attention and the processing of sensory input.

The effect seems to be more noticeable in older people, which is especially good news because it's the reverse of what typically happens as we age—gray matter usually becomes thinner. The result is consistent with other research that shows an increase in the thickness of the music areas of the brain in musicians (as was described in an article from the *Journal of Neuroscience* by Christian Gaser and Gottfried Schlaug) and the visual-motor areas of the brain in jugglers. As it is in those cases, the key is consistent practice over time.

Changing Gene Expression: Another unexpected research finding is that controlled breathing can alter the expression of genes involved in immune function, energy metabolism, and insulin secretion. The study uncovering this finding (by Bhasin et al.) was coauthored by none other than Herbert Benson himself, some forty years after he brought controlled breathing into the spotlight with his book.

And this isn't the first study linking controlled breathing to changes in genetic expression. Benson was also involved in a 2008 study (by Dusek et al.) indicating that long-term practice of the relaxation response results in changes to the expression of genes associated with how the body reacts to stress.

So that's the first technique—belly breathing. You can use this anywhere, anytime. It really works, and now you know the science to support it, too.

CALMING MUSIC

Another technique that I love is listening to calming music. Whether you have it on in the background at the office or intentionally create several times during the day that you listen to calming music, it is one of the easiest ways to create calm and relaxed concentration. You can combine it with belly breathing for amazing results. You might be wondering what type of music to choose—my suggestion is anything that seems to be relaxing to you at the time. You could create a playlist of your favorites on your device, phone, or streaming platform.

Another type of music that people have found to be calming is binaural beats music. Basically, binaural "two ears" beats are when a beat at one wavelength is played in one ear, and a beat at a different sine wavelength is played in the other ear. The difference is perceived in the brain, and has been related to a relaxation response. The research is still out on this, but I do find that it is helpful for relaxation and is definitely worth a try (although I do not recommend binaural beats if you have a seizure condition).

SETTING INTENTIONS

The third technique that I want to share is really powerful as well: setting intentions. When I present this at workshops and to my clients, they find this to be really helpful. Simple and effective—that's my favorite kind of technique!

The way you do it is to take a few deep breaths and close your eyes. Create your intention and say out loud (or at least whisper—use your voice in some way):

"My intention for the next _____ (hour, minute, patient, conversation, etc.) is _____."

The more you can really settle into this and reflect on it, even if it's only for a minute, the more you will get profound results. Again, this is a technique that can be used anywhere, any time. For example, you can set an intention when you get up that your day will be smooth. You can set an intention when you get to work that you will drink water, eat lunch, and take breaks regularly. Or, that you will have a great dinner conversation with your kids. The possibilities are endless here.

So . . . go ahead and write one down now.

"My intention for the next _____ (hour, minute, patient, conversation, etc.) is _____."

Chapter 9

EMOTIONAL FITNESS

*Our emotions have a mind of their own,
one which can hold views quite
independently of our rational mind.*

—**Daniel Goleman,**
*Emotional Intelligence:
Why It Can Matter More Than IQ*

What I call emotional fitness in the Physician Vitality System has its roots in the research on developing emotional intelligence. Emotional Intelligence (EQ or EI) is a term created by two researchers—Peter Salavoy and John Mayer—and popularized by Dan Goleman in his 1996 book of the same name. Emotional intelligence is the ability to recognize, understand, and manage our own emotions and to recognize, understand, and influence the emotions of others.

However, in the Physician Vitality System we go one step further. We not only recognize, understand, and manage our own emotions, we also learn to program and control them so that we are not buffeted by the winds of our emotions. Most people think that they do not have control over their thoughts and feelings, and that leaves them feeling like a victim and out of control in their own lives. Learning emotional fitness is an extremely powerful tool. In practical terms, this means being aware that emotions can drive our behavior and impact people (positively and negatively) and learning how to manage those emotions—both our own and others—especially when we are under pressure.

Before we get started with the techniques, I want to invite you to look at learning these techniques from a whole new perspective—and that is that you absolutely, positively *do* have the power to manage your thoughts and emotions. So many people do not really have an awareness of this truth. You won't be subject to whatever may come anymore—you will be able to handle whatever comes at you in a much better way. Because when you think about it—we are motivated by our emotions.

Advertisers know this—they associate their products with a feeling—don't they? Take an ad for water or something. You see the beautiful person by the pool or watching the sunset, drinking the water. You'll be attractive if you drink this type of water—what? How did we come to that conclusion?

We already do things to give us the emotions that we want—we just aren't necessarily conscious about it. We already do things that will "make" us feel good or feel better. We wear certain clothes, jewelry, or perfume because it makes us feel good or because it's comfortable, which makes us feel good. Our favorite chair, our coffee or tea in the morning, our favorite cup—we choose it because it makes us feel good.

That makes you a powerful person! That knowledge alone can help you to bring your stress level down so that you can feel calmer and happier. People get caught up in their emotions all the time and say things like: "I'm stressed because of that deadline," or "You made me feel angry," or "I'm upset because I have gum on my shoe." But you don't have to keep those upset feelings and thoughts. You can manage them. Managing your thoughts and emotions will give you a clearer head and less stress and make you a leader in your own life, instead of being controlled by whatever is happening around you at any given time. Make sense? So write that down . . . you absolutely, positively have the power to manage your thoughts and emotions.

How you feel about things and react to things is really just learned behavior. We have a thought, which creates a feeling, and then we take action based upon those thoughts and feelings. That's it. Once you understand that, you have so much power! I have shown you how to manage your reactions in your body and create good feelings and thoughts in the other chapters. I'm going to share with you in this chapter how to hone in more on your thoughts as they relate to your emotions, and teach you how to directly, intentionally create your day around your emotional life.

The place to begin is to first be aware of and pay attention to your emotional state. Just tune in to see how you are feeling as you go through your day. That awareness alone is a powerful first step. As you become more aware of what is happening with your emotions, you can change your emotional state if it is not helping you, for example if you are feeling anxious or stressed. I'm going to teach you how to do that in this chapter.

The three techniques that I am going to share with you are noticing your thoughts, programming your day, and cultivating positive thoughts through gratitude. I'll explain each one, both how to do it and why it works. These techniques are not fancy—they are very doable. These techniques must be practiced and used regularly to be effective, so it doesn't make sense to get complicated. It makes sense to take what works and learn that.

NOTICING YOUR THOUGHTS

The basis of this is in mindfulness therapy or third wave therapy, which is an extension of cognitive behavioral therapy or CBT. This is the premise that while we have a lot of thoughts, we don't have to pay attention to all of them, just the ones that are good or help us. We can let the other ones float away.

This is how to do it:

Set a timer for five minutes. During this time, just get quiet and start tuning in to your thoughts. When you notice that you are having a negative thought, just notice it and envision it floating away like smoke. Thoughts are just like clouds. They are just thoughts. So, for right now, just practice. Just notice your thoughts. If you are having a positive thought, such as "this is really great! I'm going to use this technique!" keep it. If you are having a negative thought, such as "I can't learn this technique," let it float away.

That's it! Simple, yet so powerful.

For most people, just recognizing the negative thoughts and acknowledging them without judgment takes a fair amount of practice in letting go. Don't get discouraged. Practice for a few minutes at a time a few times per day.

If you get good at this, then you can progress by using this technique along with some belly breathing. Breathe in the negative thought ("I am breathing in anxiety," for example) and then gently exhale the thought ("I am exhaling the anxiety"). The primary power of this technique is in really recognizing the thoughts, being nonjudgmental about them, and letting them drift away.

PROGRAMMING YOUR DAY

The next technique is called programming your day. This is one of my favorite techniques. You can really use your imagination here—and I love to use my imagination! I hope you do, too! This technique is fun!

Programming your day is a five-minute process by which you envision what you want your day to look like from an emotional point of view. So many times we get up in the morning and are just worrying from the get-go. We're thinking about work, or the kids, or our to-do list. Thinking about all of that stuff is great, but just randomly thinking doesn't often help us emotionally. It can create anxiety.

So, consciously programming your day in an emotional way makes sense, doesn't it? You are simply being intentional about how you would like your day to be. So how would you like your day to be? Easy? Happy? Do you have something planned that you would like to go well? Do you want to feel more love in your life? Feel more powerful? Do you want to feel clear-headed? Energetic? Persuasive? Intelligent? Calm? Relaxed? Courageous? Healthier? Playful?

Let's get into how to craft how we want our day to feel . . . not what we want to happen, but how we want to feel during our day.

I want you to take a minute here to think and write down an emotion that you want to feel. Just one. Let's keep this simple: _____

Did you write down one emotion that you want to feel? Great. For this exercise, I chose confidence. What did you choose? Now that you have the emotion that you want to feel, you are going to put that into a statement such as "Today I will feel confident."

So write that down—"Today I will feel _____."

And last, you are going to take a minute and feel what your emotion that you chose feels like. Close your eyes and really feel and envision it. For my example, I am feeling confident, so I would imagine what confident feels like, and I would remember a time where I felt confident. I felt great, dressed great, looked great, and was prepared . . . I knew that things were going to go my way—I just knew it! Maybe you don't have a history with it, but you can still use your imagination to feel the emotion.

So that's it! 1) Choose an emotion for the day. 2) Say out loud (but to yourself is okay) "today I will feel _____." 3) Imagine and call up that emotion until you really feel it.

I recommend doing this for at least ten minutes, but five minutes can work. It doesn't take long, but you need to be intentional about it. You need to feel that shift in your emotions.

A good way to remember to do this is to pick an anchor—something that you do every day to associate this with. Maybe you pick your emotion and make your intention before you get into the shower and then use your imagination in the shower. Maybe while your coffee is brewing. Maybe while brushing your teeth, or when you get into the car, or are waiting for the bus or the train.

CULTIVATING POSITIVE THOUGHTS THROUGH GRATITUDE

Have you noticed how this dovetails with developing inspiration as well? As was described in the previous chapter on inspiration, one of the easiest ways to connect with our hearts and spirits is to notice what is going on around us and be grateful for it. One way to start is to just be grateful that we are alive; that we have the eyesight, the brain, and the knowledge to be able to understand this book and the teachings in it; that we have the strength to be able to hold the book; etc. I'll let you take it from here.

Chapter 10

CARING FOR YOUR BODY

*Take care of your body. It's the
only place you have to live.*

—Jim Rohn

Optimizing the health and function of our bodies is key to maintaining our energy, vitality, and capacity for living the lives that we dream about—lives filled with joy and purpose. Our bodies and minds are the instrument through which we translate our thoughts, feelings, aspirations, and inspirations into reality. Our bodies and minds are in a symbiotic relationship—a true mind-body connection. It's harder to have energetic, inspired action if our bodies are not healthy. Caring for our health is one of the first things to be dropped when we get busy, but we can mitigate the fatigue that comes with being busy, stressed, or tired by caring for our bodies.

The first thing to consider when we think about a plan for physical health is kind of hiding in plain sight for a lot of us—and that is to have a personal physician ourselves and go see them annually! Even as physicians, we are just like other people and need to get checkups too, and we know that preventative care is the best care. For those of us who are feeling burned out, checking in with another physician will allow them to check for other causes that mimic the symptoms of burnout, such as thyroid problems, vitamin deficiency, adrenal fatigue, and depression. Having those regular checkups, mammograms, Pap smears, and (if you are of that age) screenings for colon cancer will also give you some peace of mind. And last but not least, you can get some help and encouragement from one of your colleagues about making any of the changes that are suggested here in this chapter.

SLEEP/ADEQUATE REST

It's like your mom told you—getting enough sleep is really important. Most of us are not getting enough sleep. How do you know? If you are sleeping in on the weekend, then you are not getting enough sleep during the week. Sleep expert Dr. Roger Washington has proposed that we go to sleep when we first feel sleepy and start to yawn—which is way earlier than most of us typically go to bed! Have you ever gone through a period of time where you are stressed and not getting enough sleep, and you do well during that stressful period, but soon after the stress is over, you get sick? Dr. Washington proposes that it isn't the stress itself that causes the illness, because oftentimes during those periods you don't just feel stress. You also feel alive, in action somehow. But you dig into your reserves, too, and you don't sleep as much or as well. What is causing the predisposition to illness is the lack of sleep. Lack of sleep has been related to autoimmune disease, mental illness, and car accidents. Did you know that staying up twenty-four hours diminishes your mental capacity in the same way as a blood alcohol level of 0.1? Think about that the next time you drive home after being on call.

While we are talking about sleep, it should be acknowledged that a lot of us have trouble getting to sleep. Sleep hygiene is really important here. It's been suggested that we turn off our screens at least two hours before bedtime. Switch to reading a book or journaling if it's not too agitating. Playing quiet music, keeping the lights low, and having a comfortable bed with your favorite things around you helps. Get rid of the television in the bedroom or cover it. And turn off your smartphone, or at least put it on *do not disturb* mode.

Have you noticed that you wake up in the same state of mind that you had when you were going to sleep? If you go to sleep worried, you wake up worried. I certainly noticed that in my patients when I was practicing Anesthesiology. That's one reason why, before they received any medication or went to sleep, I tried to make the operating room as quiet and peaceful as possible. You can use the same principles for yourself.

One way to settle down and calm our racing minds before we go to sleep is to do a "brain dump," where you take a notebook and simply write down all of the things that are going through your head at the time before you go to bed. You can also add your to-do list for the next day so that you aren't holding onto those thoughts through the night while you're sleeping.

NUTRITION/HEALTHY MEALS AND SNACKS

As we all know, our bodies do not run as well without proper nutrition. Choosing healthy foods to eat, primarily whole foods, and remembering to eat regularly can be instrumental in replenishing and renewing our energy. There have been many studies on optimal diet, and I won't go in depth here, but it has been universally accepted that a primarily plant-based diet with enough healthy fats and proteins is ideal for optimal health. The first American woman winner of the Boston Marathon in forty years, Shalane Flanigan, is still running strong at thirty-six years old, and she attributes her ability to continue to compete in marathons at a high level to her diet, which is very healthful.

As far as supplements go, I recommend a daily multivitamin with iron for everyone. Omega–3 fatty acid supplementation is helpful for some people that have stress and anxiety. The research has been mixed in terms of dosage and efficacy, but it is worth a try at two grams per day. In addition, I recommend B complex, pantothenic acid, and vitamin C to support adrenal health. And for those of us who are likely to be vitamin D deficient, adding vitamin D during the cloudy or winter months is usually a good thing to do. However, it's best to be tested specifically for deficiency before treating oneself with vitamin D.

BRIEF AND REGULAR BREAKS DURING THE DAY

Many of us motor through our day without taking scheduled breaks. However, scheduled breaks not only increase our productivity and clear our brain, they also allow us to incorporate other practices that I have already described in this book, such as meditation practices, gratitude, taking a quick walk to be in nature, connecting with a friend, colleague, or family member, or noting our emotional state or our thoughts and changing them if they are not serving us.

Here's a simple way to incorporate taking breaks into the day: if you're in the office seeing patients, you can decide that maybe every third or fourth patient you take a five-minute break. Or, if you're working at your desk, you can work for fifty or fifty-five minutes and then take a five- or ten-minute break every hour or two. You shouldn't be sitting longer than two hours without taking a break anyway, because it's bad for your circulation and posture.

Another way to take scheduled breaks is to use a method called the Pomodoro method, which is where, when you have a task that you are working on, you set a timer for a specific period of time in which you work very productively. The original timing for the Pomodoro method is taking a break at twenty-five minutes. Interestingly, the method is called the Pomodoro method because it was developed by an Italian, Francesco Cirillo, in the 1980s; the group was using a timer that looked like a tomato, and Pomodoro is Italian for tomato.

In any case, the concept is that as you're working on a specific task, you schedule a specific amount of time where you will work diligently and then, when the timer goes off, you stop and take a break. For example, as I was working on this book chapter, I estimated how many "Pomodoros" it would take to complete this task. You can also use this technique to plan your day. First prioritize the tasks you need to do, estimating the amount of time they take, and then calculate how many "Pomodoros" it takes to complete the task that you have in front of you.

REGULAR EXERCISE

This is one of my favorite things to talk about when I speak at workshops or with clients. I truly believe that regular exercise is the elixir of life. If we continue regular exercise throughout our lifetime, it promotes our health and wellbeing and has been shown to improve our quality of life dramatically. My experience has been that going to the gym and exercising with others has been a great way for me to socialize and make friends, as we have something healthy in common.

I'm often asked about what type of physical exercise is the best. I have my own things that I like to do, but you have to do what YOU like to do, or else you will not do it. It's unlikely that you will keep doing something that you don't like to do, so choosing something that you don't like doesn't make any sense. My advice is simple—choose one or two things that you would like doing and then stick with that regularly. I think of it in terms of how one might get kids involved in physical activity, since we are kids at heart. If you like walking, walk. If you like running, run. Whatever you like to do, do it regularly. But remember, it's important to make sure that you have a combination of aerobic exercise, strength training, and stretching.

You should exercise at least four to five days a week, at least thirty minutes per day—and not just aerobic exercise such as walking, running, biking, or (my favorite by far) dance fitness. It's also important to include at least one to two sessions of strength training per week, especially for women. If you are not familiar with strength training, hire a trainer to teach you the safe way to train, and then go for it!

We tend to underestimate the value of strength training, even though we know that it helps to minimize injury and decrease the likelihood of osteoporosis. Heavy weightlifting has been underemphasized for women, but it has been shown to be the most effective way to increase the strength, size, and appearance of our muscles. So, if you want to be stronger and faster, and fit into your clothes better, then heavy lifting is the way to go. My personal routine is to lift as heavy as possible with good form, no more than eight to ten reps per set.

I am a huge fan of dance fitness (Zumba and WERQ), and I can't tell you how instrumental it has been in my life over the last six or seven years to keep me healthy and sane as I have gone through various personal challenges. Even when I travel, I will try to attend class, and it's fun to meet new people in different cities. For me, dance fitness doesn't feel like exercise at all—it's so much fun. You get over your inhibitions about moving your body, and I have made so many friends in my Zumba and WERQ classes. I just can't say enough about them. I'm even certified to teach both formats!

Bonus

YOUR PHYSICIAN VITALITY SELF-TEST

When doctors have joy, vitality, and purpose in their lives, they are better doctors and they do not suffer from physician burnout. Are you feeling burned out?

How *is* life going for you these days? Are you feeling healthy? Energetic? Positive about your work? Do you feel joy every day? This self-test will help you to easily see where things are going well and where there are opportunities to create more of what you want in your life.

Go to www.drdianne.com to take the test.

REFERENCES

Bhasin, M. K., J. A. Dusek, B. Chang, M. G. Joseph, J. W. Denninger, G. L. Fricchione, H. Benson, and T. A. Libermann. "Relaxation Response Induces Temporal Transcriptome Changes in Energy Metabolism, Insulin Secretion and Inflammatory Pathways." *PLoS ONE* 8(5): e62817. doi:10.1371/journal.pone.0062817.

Dusek, J. A., H. H. Otu, A. L. Wohlhueter, M. Bhasin, L. F. Zerbini, M. G. Joseph, H. Benson, and T. A. Libermann. "Genomic Counter-Stress Changes Induced by the Relaxation Response." *PLoS ONE* 3(7): e2576. doi:10.1371/journal.pone.0002576.

Gaser, C., and G. Schlaug. "Brain Structures Differ between Musicians and Non-Musicians." *Journal of Neuroscience* 23, no. 27 (8 October 2003): 9240–45.

Schwartz, Tony, and Catherine McCarthy. "Manage Your Energy, Not Your Time." *Harvard Business Review*, October 2007. https://hbr.org/2007/10/manage-your-energy-not-your-time.

FURTHER RESOURCES

The Power of Rest: Why Sleep Alone Is Not Enough by Matthew Edlund, MD. (Harper One Publishers.)

Nonprofit Transformed by Cathy Phelps, MA, LCSW. (McIntire Publishing Services.)

Lack of Sufficient Sleep Matters: Decode the Root Cause of Your Illness by Roger W. Washington, MD. (CreateSpace Independent Publishing Platform.)

To learn more about the vagus nerve and your heart, go to www.heartmath.com.

Read more about binaural beats in the article "Auditory Beat Stimulation and Its Effects on Cognition and Mood States" by Leila Chaieb et al. from *Frontiers in Psychiatry* journal: https://www.ncbi.nlm.nih.gov/pmc/articles/PMC4428073/

ABOUT THE AUTHOR

Dianne Ansari-Winn is a board certified Anesthesiologist and nationally recognized author, speaker, and coach. She is the founder of the Physician Vitality Institute and The Physician Coaching Academy, where she teaches physicians how to coach and guide other physicians. As a doctor herself, Dianne has a unique insight into the challenges that her clients face and guides them with compassion, grace, and humor to the lives that they want, with optimum health in mind, body, and spirit. She has also created a unique platform for her fellow doctors to share their expertise, including personal health and wellbeing, through her podcast, *The Doctor's Life*.

Dr. Dianne's mission is to create a new paradigm in healthcare where physician wellness is considered to be an integral part of medical practice. She believes that better healthcare is inevitable when physicians have health, energy, joy, and fulfillment, and works to help doctors heal the world.

To learn more, visit www.drdianne.com

CREATING DISTINCTIVE BOOKS
WITH INTENTIONAL RESULTS

We're a collaborative group of creative masterminds
with a mission to produce high-quality books to position
you for monumental success in the marketplace.

Our professional team of writers, editors, designers,
and marketing strategists work closely together to ensure
that every detail of your book is a clear representation
of the message in your writing.

Want to know more?
Write to us at info@publishyourgift.com
or call (888) 949-6228

Discover great books, exclusive offers, and more at
www.PublishYourGift.com

Connect with us on social media

@publishyourgift

CPSIA information can be obtained
at www.ICGtesting.com
Printed in the USA
FSHW021858130419
57234FS

9 781949 134988